Playing with Light and Shadows

by Jennifer Boothroyd

first step nonfiction

Lerner Publications Company · Minneapolis

LERNER

SOURCE™

Expand learning beyond the printed book. Download free, complementary educational resources for this book from our website, www.lernersource.com.

The images in this book are used with the permission of: © iStockphoto.com/CEFutcher, p. 4; © Beata Becla/Shutterstock.com, p. 5; © iStockphoto.com/RBFried, p. 6; © iStockphoto.com/isitsharp, p. 7; © iStockphoto.com/Meinzahn, p. 8; © iStockphoto.com/grapegeek, p. 9; © iStockphoto.com/suzyco, p. 10; © MarcelC/iStock/Thinkstock, p. 11; © iStockphoto.com/aroax, p. 12; © iStockphoto.com/ RonfromYork, p. 13; © Dimijana/iStock/Thinkstock, p. 14; © Jupiterimages/Photos.com/Thinkstock, p. 15; © iStockphoto.com/PeskyMonkey, p. 16; © iStockphoto.com/mikkean, p. 17; © Gary John Norman/Taxi/Getty Images, p. 18; © Geri Lavrov/Photographer's Choice/Getty Images, p. 19; © Fuse/Thinkstock, p. 20; © ULTRA.F/The Image Bank/Getty Images, p. 21; © iStockphoto.com/ travnikovstudio, p. 22.

Front Cover: © Alexander Kladoff/iStock/Thinkstock

Main body text set in ITC Avant Garde Gothic Std Medium 21/25.
Typeface provided by Adobe Systems.

Lerner Publications Company
A division of Lerner Publishing Group, Inc.
241 First Avenue North
Minneapolis, MN 55401 USA

For reading levels and more information, look up this title at www.lernerbooks.com.

Library of Congress Cataloging-in-Publication Data

Cataloging-in-Publication Data for *Playing with Light and Shadows* is on file at the Library of Congress.
ISBN: 978–1–4677–3912–2 (LB)
ISBN: 978–1–4677–4686–1 (EB)

Manufactured in the United States of America
2 – CG – 3/1/16

Table of Contents

Light and Shadows

Light is all around us.

Light falls on the objects
we see.

What is that dark shape
on the ground?   It is a
shadow.

The boys are blocking the sunlight.

A shadow forms where light is blocked.

Blocking Light

Some materials are **opaque**. They block all light that hits them.

The swing has a shadow.

Shadows form behind opaque objects.

9

Some materials are
translucent.

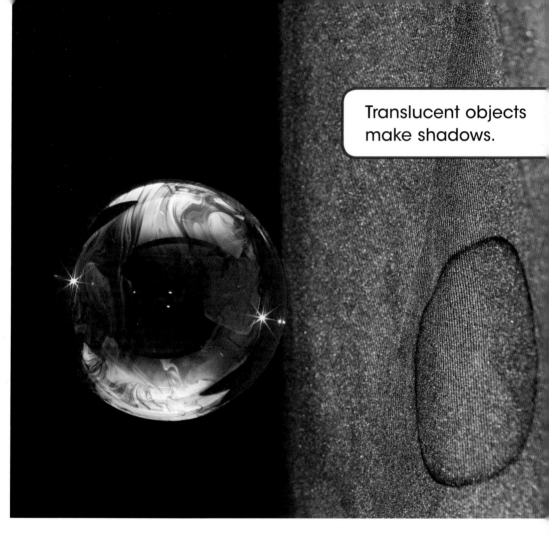

Translucent objects make shadows.

They block some light. But some light passes through.

Transparent materials let all light pass through. No shadows form.

The glass is transparent.

The window frame makes a shadow. The glass does not.

This shadow looks stretched.

In the morning, shadows are long.

At noon, shadows are very
short.

In the evening, shadows are long again.

You can make shadows!

Stand outside in the sun.

Make shadow puppets with your hands.

How else can you block light?

Glossary

opaque – not letting any light
   through

shadow – a dark area made
   when light is blocked

translucent – letting some
   light through

transparent – letting all light
   through

Index